9

W9-BCF-069

The Year of Our Revolution

The Year of Our Revolution

New and Selected Stories and Poems

Judith Ortiz Cofer

PIÑATA BOOKS
ARTE PÚBLICO PRESS
HOUSTON, TEXAS
1998

This volume is made possible through grants from the National Endowment for the Arts (a federal agency), Andrew W. Mellon Foundation, and the City of Houston through The Cultural Arts Council of Houston, Harris County.

Piñata Books are full of surprises!

Piñata Books
An Imprint of Arte Público Press
University of Houston
Houston, Texas 77204-2090

Cover illustration and design by James F. Brisson

Ortiz Cofer, Judith
    The year of our revolution: New and selected stories and poems / by Judith Ortiz Cofer.
    p.   cm.
    ISBN 1-55885-224-7 (cloth : alk. paper)
    1. Hispanic Americans—Literary collections. [1. Hispanic Americans—Literary collections.] I. Title.
PZ7.0765Yg   1998
[Fic]—dc21   98-13097
                                                                        CIP
                                                                        AC

Some of the material contained herein has been previously published. Acknowledgements of previous publication are made on page 101, which constitutes an extension of this page. All material copyright © Judith Ortiz Cofer.

⊚ The paper used in this publication meets the requirements of the American National Standard for Information Sciences—Permanence of Paper for Printed Library Materials, ANSI Z39.48-1984.

8 9 0 1 2 3 4 5 6 7   10 9 8 7 6 5 4 3 2 1

For my family, here and on the Island

Take me disappearin' through the smoke rings of my mind,
Down the foggy ruins of time . . .
—Bob Dylan, "Mister Tambourine Man"

Contents

*O*rigen

What we want to know:
In the unimaginable moment
of the union of parental flesh,
was there love, or
are we the heirs of carelessness?
This matters,
That we were wanted; called forth
to fulfill a wish.
That we were meant to be.

$\mathcal{V}$olar

At twelve I was an avid consumer of comic books—*Supergirl* being my favorite. I spent my allowance of a quarter a day on two twelve-cent comic books or a double issue for twenty-five. I had a stack of *Legion of Super Heroes* and *Supergirl* comic books in my bedroom closet that was as tall as I. I had a recurring dream in those days: that I had long blonde hair and could fly. In my dream I climbed the stairs to the top of our apartment building as myself, but as I went up each flight, changes would be taking place. Step by step I would fill out: my legs would grow long, my arms harden into steel, and my hair would magically go straight and turn a golden color. Of course, I would add the bonus of breasts, but not too large; Supergirl had to be aerodynamic, and sleek and hard as a supersonic missile. Once on the roof, my parents safely asleep in their beds, I would get on tip-toe, arms outstretched in the position for flight, and jump out of my fifth-story-high window into the black lake of the sky. From up there, over the rooftops, I could see everything, even beyond the few blocks of our barrio; with my x-ray vision I could look inside the homes of people who interested me.

Once I saw our landlord, whom I knew my parents feared, sitting in a treasure-room dressed in an ermine coat and a large gold crown. He sat on the floor counting his dollar bills. I played a trick on him. Going up to his building's chimney, I blew a little puff of my super-breath into his fireplace, scattering his stacks of money so that he had to start counting all over again.

I could more or less program my Supergirl dreams in those days by focusing on the object of my current obsession. This way I saw into the private lives of my neighbors, my teachers, and in the last days of my childish fantasy and the beginning of adolescence, into the secret rooms of the boys I liked. In the mornings I'd wake up in my tiny bedroom with its incongruous—at least in our tiny apartment—white "princess" furniture my mother had chosen for me, and find myself back in my body; my tight curls still clinging to my head, my skinny arms and legs and flat chest unchanged.

In the kitchen my mother and father would be talking softly over a *café con leche*. She would come "wake me" exactly forty-five minutes after they had gotten up. It was their time together at the beginning of each day, and even at an early age I could feel their disappointment if I interrupted them by getting up too early. So I would stay in my bed recalling my dreams of flight, perhaps planning my next flight. In the kitchen they would be discussing events in the barrio. Actually, my father would be carrying that part of the conversation; when it was her turn to speak she would, more often than not, try shifting the topic toward her desire to see her *familia* on the Island: How about a vacation in Puerto Rico together this year, *querido?* We could rent a car, go to the beach. We could . . . And he would answer patiently, gently: *Mi amor,* do you know how much it would cost for all of us to fly there? It is not possible for me to take the time off . . . *Mi vida,* please understand . . . And I knew that soon she would rise from the table. Not abruptly. She would light a cigarette and look out the kitchen window. The view was of a dismal alley that was littered with refuse thrown from windows. The space was too narrow for anyone larger than a skinny child to enter safely, so it was never cleaned. My mother would check the time on the clock over her sink, the one with a prayer for patience and grace written in Spanish. A birthday gift. She would see that it was time to wake me. She'd sigh deeply and say the same thing the view from her kitchen window always inspired her to say: *"Ay, si yo pudiera volar."*

The Meaning of El Amor

1

At my father's funeral there were mostly women. They ranged in age from, I would say, mine, at eighteen, to my mother's, about twice that. They looked to me like a Greek chorus, perhaps because I had just seen a production of *Antigone* at City College as a final junior-year field trip with my class. The women—there were at least three women there I could not account for as family or friends—were dressed in black. And since this was a Puerto Rican funeral, so were most of us, but what set these women apart was their staginess. They were dressed-up for the funeral, like actresses, in full make-up, with veils. Since my father moonlighted as a master of ceremonies at a local nightclub, they might just have been part of the revue. But their tears seemed real to me. They stayed in a group as if they had something in common. I sensed strongly that their bond was, had been, my father.

My mother ignored the women and begged me with her eyes to do the same. But I couldn't tear my eyes away from them. It had been an unspoken rule at our house that we did not speak of, or even acknowledge, my father's nightlife. We spoke only of his day job as the security/maintenance man in an apartment building. What he did after 10 P.M. was not something I ever knew about until I was old enough to stay up to hear the frantic whispers exchanged by parents, and the soft, but firm, locking of the door. As I got older, people were only too eager to tell me about Paterson's Puerto Rican Romeo: janitor by day, lady-killer by night.

2

I had been trying to spend time with my mother since Papi died, but she was not cooperating. She had other plans that did not include me: Getting widow-counseling from Father Colinas, the new Spanish—from Spain—pastor of the Catholic church in our barrio. For weeks after the funeral she avoided being alone with me, claiming to have a headache or acting too tired to talk when I came home from school. After vacation started, it became clear that she did not want to talk to anyone about my father. And she did not shed a single tear, not in front of me anyway. She spent all day doing volunteer work with other women at the church. It was what she has wanted all those years, she seemed to be telling the world, to do her charity work and go to church anytime she wanted without having to explain it to her husband. His joke had been that when they met she really wanted to be Christ's bride but had settled for him. They were as mismatched as a man and a woman could be. She smelled like incense, and he like Puerto Rican rum.

After school ended, I found myself with lots of free time, since I hadn't tried to get a summer job, thinking she'd want me around for company when the shock of his death finally hit her. I really thought that the same thing that was happening to me would happen to her. I had felt sort of in a daze the whole time, from when the police came to the door at 2 A.M. to tell us that Papi had collapsed backstage at the Caribbean Moon and had been taken to Memorial Hospital, where he had been pronounced DOA from a massive coronary, to the funeral my mother's church friends arranged.

It was like it was happening outside of me. I kept telling myself, Papi is dead, Papi is dead. Sometimes I said it in Spanish, which sounded more dramatic somehow: *Papi está muerto.* But it didn't really sink in until I saw her cleaning out his closet and sealing all his things in boxes. She did it all like it was regular house-cleaning. His fancy suits with the satin lapels and pockets, which the club had sent in plastic bags, she folded and put in a box marked for the Salvation Army. His work clothes she put in one labeled *Iglesia.* I guess she was too ashamed of his nightclub outfits to send them to the church for their bazaar. She was dividing up his life like she had always done.

Standing at the door watching her make my father's life disappear into neat packages made me angry, and when I spoke, she jumped up from the kneeling position she had been in, startled by my voice. She stumbled and hit her elbow on the night table. I saw the look of intense pain pass over her face and I thought, *Good, maybe now she'll cry, even if it's just for herself.* But she didn't. What I had said without thinking was: "Why did you marry him?" She stared at me for what seemed like a long time, then she looked down at the box with the tuxedos and red bow-ties in it.

"I believed that I could change him. That I could help save him," she said in a flat voice. Then she went back down on her knees and continued sealing boxes and labeling them.

That's when I shut myself up in my room and cried like I hadn't cried since I was a little child and she had punished me with her silences. I knew I was alone then. Not that Papi had been there much for me, but he had allowed me to believe that there was another world outside our apartment that maybe someday I would discover. And I did. To add to my despair, my father's secret world was as miserable in my eyes as my mother's religious obsessions. Now that he was gone, I had nothing to do but try to figure out whether there was anything I could learn about my father's life that would help me deal with it and allow me to go on with mine. To me he had been the handsome visitor I saw briefly at dinner time, between day and night jobs. At the table, all conversation was directed and censored by my mother, who steered all talk away from her long list of forbidden subjects, father's job at the nightclub being at the top.

But as soon as I turned eighteen I violated the primary rule at our house. One evening, claiming to have a last-minute assignment to do at the library, I took the bus downtown to the Caribbean Moon. With make-up I could look as old as I wanted, and I walked in like a regular customer. It's in the attitude, anyway. Nobody asked questions. The place was much smaller than I had imagined a nightclub would be. Really no more than one poorly lit room with a bar at the back.

It smelled of stale beer and worse, like a warehouse that hadn't been aired out in years.

I decided to find a seat in the back. I slid into a booth and felt my stockings tear on the rough vinyl. The top of the table was sticky, so I kept my hands in my lap. I watched an old man setting up the bar. A woman about my mother's age, but wearing a ridiculous short skirt with ruffled panties, leaned over tables lighting what looked like yellow bug-candles. I thought she'd be able to tell my age or would ask me for my ID. But other customers started filing in, and she greeted each man loudly by name, then went to place their drink orders at the bar. I slid to the end of the seat next to the wall, where I thought no one could see me without coming very close. Several women came in and sat on the stools at the bar. I thought I recognized at least one from our building. She lived alone and called my father at least once a week to go fix something that went wrong at her place. I think her name was Mercedes, but my mother called her La Fulana—what you call someone who doesn't deserve a name. "La Fulana is on the phone for you," she would always say to my father, handing him the receiver with two fingers as if it were a dirty thing. Some salsa music blared out from the juke box for a little while, and some of the men at the tables went over to the women at the bar. There was a re-shuffling as the couples then migrated to tables together.

Then the lights went down and from the farthest booth in the back I saw my father come on stage in his light blue tuxedo with wide black lapels. Everything shone on him, from his shoes that reflected the spotlight like black stars to his thick mustache and wavy hair. He was a different man from the one who came home around six in the evening, wearing the gray coveralls of a janitor and smelling of ammonia and floor wax. I did not want to startle him by revealing myself too soon. I would wait until after the show and tell him that I had been watching and that I was very proud of him. I felt entirely confident that he would be glad that I had disobeyed Mother. My usual method of deciding what each of my parents would like or dislike was to simply think in opposite terms: whatever my mother held sacred, my father mocked, and those things that father loved, my mother found wasteful, sinful, or profane.

"Tito," she would say when he'd come out of their room on a Saturday night dressed in a flashy guayabera and smelling as if he had bathed in Aqua Velva, when she and I would be heading for a prayer service or a PG movie at the Imperial, and he the Caribbean Moon or elsewhere.

"You are teaching our daughter the Devil's ways by your example," she would admonish, pointing her finger at him.

"And you, *mi amor,* have a heavenly multitude behind you," he would laugh, slapping her bottom, as he walked past us to the door. "Isabel has nothing to fear when you have her by her little hand." Then he'd wink at me and be gone.

It is safe to say that my father and I remained strangers under my mother's strict vigilance all those years. I always wanted to know more about him, and when she was working in the kitchen I would sometimes go into their room and look in his side of the closet. He must have kept all his performing clothes at the club. I never saw anything more extraordinary than an old black tuxedo jacket. One time I dug out a long cigarette holder from its pocket and imagined him dressed like Clark Gable in a movie, blowing perfect circles of smoke out into an adoring audience in a glittering place where he was the King of the Night. Mother did not allow him to smoke in our apartment. But, as much as she criticized the way he dressed, she slaved over his shirts and pants, ironing them with manic determination into perfection. Yet she hated the way he dressed in loud colors and two-toned shoes. She herself wore loose skirts, plain cotton blouses, and flat shoes. I had to wear what she told me, but found my own ways to rebel, taking clothes I bought for myself with baby-sitting money in my school bag and changing in the girl's lavatory before and after school. As I got older I also decided that I wanted to know more about Papi.

The year before he died was especially bad between my mother and me. I had met a boy I wanted to go out with and she had put her foot down because he was a Protestant, and besides I was too young to be messing around with boys, she said. I snuck out to see him anyway. She was so involved in church and barrio activities that I could always get out to see Hector. He lived in our building and his mother, Doña Caridad, liked me and encouraged me to come over to their place. Hector and I didn't last long together. Nobody's fault, he just ended up boring me. All he talked about was baseball. But I began to really see my mother as a sad and angry person. It was like she didn't believe two people could be happy together. So, I decided to try to talk to Papi. But first I wanted to see for myself what his other life, his night world, was like. I imagined it as the opposite of my mother's dreary routines. Glamour. Beautiful people. That's what I thought Papi went to when he left our apartment at night.

3

That night at the Caribbean Moon I sat in the shadows where he couldn't see me but I could see him. He was in a room near the kitchen behind me, and through the open door I saw and heard him discussing the night's program with a young black man he called Mano. They spoke in Spanish and I recognized Mano's accent as Cuban. I envied the easy talk they exchanged. At home, conversation was always guarded. I do not remember Mother ever laughing out loud at his jokes, which she considered in bad taste usually. But here he said some things to the Cuban man that made my cheeks burn, but I enjoyed hearing him laugh so freely.

When the waiter came, I ordered a glass of wine. My first non-sacramental wine ever. It was sweet as grape juice. Then the red velvet curtain went up and I sat back to watch my father introduce the first act. He radiated charm as he spoke in Spanish into the microphone. He told a joke about a man with an unfaithful wife who was asked by his friends why he put up with it. "She is not made of soap, she will not wear out," the husband had replied. Some customers laughed a little. I did not get it. But it turned out to have been my father's little prelude to the first performance of the evening.

To a drum roll, a big woman he called Lady Palmolive was wheeled out in a tub full of bubbles to the middle of the stage. There she drew Tito to her, after calling to him by drawing his name out into a high note like a dog baying at the moon. She gave him a loud popping kiss on the mouth that reverberated through the small place. She began singing a Spanish song made up mostly of obscene references to the female anatomy. Then, most incongruously, a recording of Bobby Darin's "Splish, Splash" blasted out, and two other women wearing nothing but towels ran on stage. They handed Lady Palmolive a towel while pirouetting around her so the audience got glimpses of a large amount of flesh. Then the three did a fast-paced number maneuvering their towels to expose a buttock or a breast. It was amateurish and vulgar.

By the time my father returned to his microphone to announce a little break, while "the ladies dry off and you men out there go take cold showers—just kidding, *amigos*," I was getting my things together to leave. I was not angry then, just very disappointed and a little disgusted. I could not face him. It would embarrass both of us. My main emotion was sadness that my father had either settled for or come to this. He was intelligent. He had to know how demeaning his work was.

When I started my senior year at Eastside High, my life at home became secondary to my interest in this other world that had opened up to me. I had a crush on a boy who had just transferred from California. Pablo was Chicano, and the best-looking boy I had ever seen. His skin was the color of a new penny and although he was not too tall, his body was that of a swimmer. He told me that the main thing he missed about California was the beach. But he played guitar, so it wasn't long before he had joined a band with some Puerto Rican boys and he was making money playing at weddings and baptisms in the barrio. That's one thing you could count on back then: Nobody ever had money, but there was a fiesta every Saturday night. If it was in a good Catholic home, I was allowed to go. So I got to be with Pablo quite a bit.

But I could not stop thinking about Papi's other life, especially since my mother had built a wall between us that I found hard to live with. So after school was out and Pablo went to visit his married sister in California, I decided to visit the Caribbean Moon one more time. This time I went early and waited by the side door, through which I had seen the employees come in and out. I hid behind some empty liquor cartons, peeking out when I heard footsteps. I saw Mano come in and considered trying to talk to him, but I thought that he might get the wrong idea about me, so I decided to wait for one of the women from the act. I wanted to talk to one of the three who had come to Papi's funeral. If they cared enough to do that, I thought they might let me ask them a few questions.

Lady Palmolive was the first one to arrive. I had heard the sharp clicking of high-heeled shoes from a distance and had taken a deep breath. What if I was wrong to do this? This was a bad neighborhood and a bad crowd. What if they called my mother to tell her I was there, or the police? But I had to know about Papi, or I would never have peace or a chance to understand what made him be the way he had been. So I jumped out of my hiding place as Lady P came up to the door. She let out a high-pitched little scream and opened her eyes real big. She was older than she looked on stage, her face was a mask of make-up, and her tired eyes were rimmed with black liner and long false eyelashes. There were long lines framing her red mouth. She scared me too. So I guess we both just stood there staring at each other before I said, "Excuse me, *permiso, por favor,* Miss Palmolive. *Lo siento.* I'm sorry I scared you." I spoke in Spanish and English, blubbering my apologies like an idiot. She just looked at me as if *I* were a strange sight. Then she grinned and shook her head.

"You scared the pee-pee out of me, *niña.*" Hearing her say *pee-pee* in a Minnie-Mouse voice made me giggle. I guess I was a little hysterical by then. I remembered hearing Lady Palmolive sing and thinking that little voice couldn't be coming out of that pink mountain of flesh. Not that she was fat. I guess you could call her very voluptuous—from the magazines I've seen in the homes of some of my friends, I know that Puerto Rican men like women with meat on their bones. At least my father's generation did.

"I'm sorry I frightened you," I repeated, trying to make my hands stop shaking.

"You are Tito's daughter, no?"

She extended her hand out toward me. Her nails were about an inch long and painted bright red. I took it thinking that it felt unnaturally soft. But I guessed she got to soak it a lot. That thought of her in a tub being dragged out onto the stage made me feel like I was going to explode in a fit of giggles, and I looked down at the ground to try to regain my self-control.

"Are you okay? You are Isabel, right? Your Papi's death must have really upset you. Come in. We'll have a drink. A cup of *café*, I mean."

I managed to nod my head and let her lead me in to the backstage of the Caribbean Moon, which was worse than the club itself. The hallway was lit by a hanging light-bulb, which swung around to reveal cracks on the yellow walls. We walked down past several doors with names written in black marker on them. One said PRIVATE, so I guessed it was the owner's or manager's, the next said TITO, and it had a hand-drawn star above it—the kind made by children all over their notebooks. Someone had placed roses on the floor in front of the door. They were dry and as we passed, petals scattered under my feet. I followed Lady P to the end of the hallway, where she entered a door painted hot pink.

"We painted it ourselves," she said as I stopped to look at the decals glued on it. They were Disney cartoon characters. She placed a red fingernail on the dancing hippopotamus from *Fantasia*. "That's me," she said and winked at me.

It was obviously a dressing room used by several women. There was a rack of costumes which filled the small space with a strong odor of sweat and perfume. In front of a long mirror worn through to the black paint on the back in several places there were folding chairs. The counter was completely covered with cosmetics, hair brushes, bottles of soda drunk down to different levels, and an assortment of medicines. I must have let my eyes linger on the tube of hemorrhoid creme a little too long, because Lady P picked it up and explained that the girls used it to reduce puffiness under their eyes. "An old model's trick one of them had read about in a magazine."

"Does it work?" I was fascinated by the place and its contents. There was nothing here I would ever think of using or wearing, unless it was to a costume party. But maybe that's what this woman's life was, a costume party.

She set up two folding chairs and led me to the one not facing the mirror.

"Sit down, *mi amor*. I have to start getting ready for my solo act. But I'll have Mano bring us some *café*."

She stuck her head out the door and yelled out to Mano that she needed two cups of coffee, *"Ahora mismo."* Right now. Her high-pitched voice carried like a whistle and echoed from the walls.

To my surprise, she stepped out of her tent dress in front of me. She was wearing a red slip.

"Lady Palmolive, I can step out while you dress," I offered, hoping she would not be offended by my shyness. No one took off their clothes in front of me at my house, and I felt that my cheeks were burning.

"I'm sorry, *niña*. I have no manners. I'll dress behind this rack here. I forget that some people have *modestia*, you know. And by the way, Lady Palmolive is not my real name. I am Bernarda López Rivera, at your service. But I cannot use that name to perform. Too proper. It was Tito, your *papi*, who thought of calling me Lady Palmolive. After the bath soap. You know, for the bathtub act."

She was talking to me from behind the clothes rack and her voice came through muffled and distant as she struggled into her costume.

"*Señora* Bernarda." I suddenly wanted to get out of the stifling room with its stale smells of women my father had known well enough to give them stage names. There was a knock at the door and an "*¡Entre!*" from behind the clothes rack.

It was Mano carrying a Pabst Blue Ribbon Beer metal tray with two cups of coffee on it. He smiled at me. "Tito's daughter." He placed a cup into my hands and nodded at me. "It's nice to see you again."

Startled at his words, I spilled some very hot coffee on my lap. I scalded my thigh. The woman came out to see what the commotion was about. I guess I must have made a noise of pain.

Mano said, "I'll get her some ice."

I was in tears, but not just from the pain. What had he meant that he was glad to see me *again?* When had he seen me?

In her ridiculous costume of terry-cloth, Bernarda sat in front of me and applied some Jergens lotion to the red spot on my thigh. I tried to make her stop. Then Mano walked in with a glass of ice and a kitchen towel. He put them on the dressing table and rushed out after taking a quick look at the burn. As he closed the door, he said, *"No es serio."*

It wasn't worth tears, I interpreted as the meaning of the "It isn't serious." I had wanted to ask him where he had seen me before.

After packing the ice in the towel, the woman handed it to me and sat back on her chair.

"Why are you here, *niña?*" Her tone had lost its playfulness. Her arms were crossed over her ample chest and her thickly outlined eyebrows had come together.

"Keep that ice on it," she said as I continued to sob uncontrollably. I suddenly felt like a child in an adult place. Something about hearing this woman say my father's name with such intimacy had made me feel very resentful, and afraid. Had he loved this awful, painted woman?

"I came to ask you about my father." I finally got myself under control. I wiped my face with the cold towel.

"He died here, he practically lived here," I said. "I want to know . . ."

"You want to know if he had a woman here, right?" She dragged her chair closer to the mirror and talked into her reflection instead of to me. "Your father spent a lot of time here, that is true. But it was not for the reasons you think."

"Why, then?" I was afraid to hear about my father's secret life in this place, but I could not go home without knowing.

"He had friends here, and fans . . . people who admired him and respected him. At home he had only criticism and rejection from your mother. She did not understand our Tito, *niña*."

"He was not your Tito, " I said with more anger than I intended. "I'm sorry," I said.

"No. You are right. He was your father. But he was our *compañero*. He loved only one woman. He wanted her to love and accept him the way he was, though. And she could not ever do that. So it was constant war. That woman was your mother."

"How do you know all this?"

"Because I . . . and this is hard for me to say to you . . . I loved Tito. I tried every way that I knew how to tempt him away from his home. But he kept thinking that one day she would change. As the years went by and things got worse at home, he started spending more and more time 'on the Moon,' he used to say, *'en la luna.'* But he was proud of the way you had turned out. He thought you had spirit and that someday you'd make something of yourself."

I had been staring at her face in the mirror. I had been preparing myself to hate this cheap nightclub dancer. Lady Palmolive, the stripper, my father's mistress. But then I saw the tears that were creating two deep streaks on her face. She was honestly grieving for my father.

"He talked about me?"

"To anyone who would listen. He had pictures of you on his dressing room walls too. Maybe they are still there. Take a look. But, *niña,* I have to get dressed for my show. And I have to start again with my make-up!" She had put on that false cheerfulness again, and I knew I was being dismissed.

"One last thing."

"I will answer one more question, *señorita.* But you will have to leave then. I am a working woman, you know."

"What did Mano mean when he said that he had seen me before?"

Bernarda put her hand under my chin and made me look into her moist eyes, blackened and smeared by make-up.

"Your father saw you that night you sat in the back booth. We all knew you were here and tried to convince him not to do the show. But he wanted you to see him as he really was. He hoped that you would talk to him."

I thanked her and walked out of the Caribbean Moon feeling confused about everything. What does love mean when you can't even talk openly to the people who are closest to you?

4

When I got home I saw that my mother was sitting at the kitchen table concentrating hard on something.

Quietly I walked up behind her. She had a set of pictures spread out like tarot cards in front of her. She was moving them around as if trying to find the right pattern. The photos showed her and Tito as a young couple, maybe on their honeymoon in Puerto Rico. There was also their wedding photo, with him looking like a movie star and her like a shy, pretty fan looking into his eyes. In the middle there was a photo of the three of us when I was a baby. Her eyes were beginning to look sad by then.

I put my hands on her shoulders and hugged her to me.

"I was just about to put these away. Before you came home."

"Did you love him?" I asked.

"He was the love of my life," she said, "*Ay, hija,* I wish that he had loved me too."

I felt her tremble and I knew that she would now be able to cry and begin to free herself from the anger, as I had. And maybe I would tell her about his "trips to the Moon," about Lady Palmolive, and why he had always come back to us.

Vida

To a child, life is a play directed by parents, teachers, and other adults who are forever giving directions: "Say this," "Don't say that," "Stand here," "Walk this way," "Wear these clothes," and on and on and on. If we miss or ignore a cue, we are punished. And so we memorized the script of our lives as interpreted by our progenitors, and we learned not to extemporize too much: The world—our audience—likes the well-made play, with everyone in their places and not too many bursts of brilliance or surprises. But once in a while new characters walk onto the stage, and the writers have to scramble to fit them in, and for a while, life gets interesting.

Vida was a beautiful Chilean girl who simply appeared in the apartment upstairs with her refugee family one day and introduced herself into our daily drama.

She was tall, thin and graceful as a ballerina, with fair skin and short black hair. She looked like a gazelle as she bounded down the stairs from her apartment to ours the day she first came to our door to borrow something. Her accent charmed us. She said that she had just arrived from Chile with her sister, her sister's newborn baby girl, her sister's husband, and their grandmother. They were all living together in a one-bedroom apartment on the floor above us.

There must have been an interesting story of political exile there, but I was too young to care about that detail. I was immediately fascinated by the lovely Vida, who looked like one of the models in the fashion magazines that I, just turning twelve, had begun to be interested in. Vida came into my life during one of my father's long absences with the Navy, so that his constant vigilance was not a hindrance to my developing attachment to this vibrant human being. It was not a friendship—she was too much older than I and too self-involved to give me much in return for my devotion. It was more a Sancho Panza/Knight of La Mancha relationship, with me following her while she explored the power of her youth and beauty.

Vida wanted to be a movie star in Hollywood. That is why she had come to America, she said. I believed that she would be, although she spoke almost no English. That was my job, she said, to teach her to speak perfect English without an accent. She had finished secondary school in her country, and although she was only sixteen, she was not going to school in Paterson. She had other plans. She would get a job as soon as she had papers, save money, then she would leave for Hollywood as soon as possible. She asked me how far Hollywood was. I showed her the state of California in my geography book. She traced a line with her finger from New Jersey to the west coast and smiled. Nothing seemed impossible to Vida.

It was summer when I met Vida, and we spent our days in the small, fenced-in square lot behind our apartment building, avoiding going indoors as much as possible, since it was depressing to Vida to hear her family talking about the need to find jobs, to smell sour baby smells, or to be constantly lectured to by her obese grandmother, who sat like a great pile of laundry on a couch all day, watching shows on television which she did not understand. The brother-in-law frightened me a little with his intense eyes and his constant pacing. He spoke in whispers to his wife, Vida's sister, when I was around, as if he did not want me to overhear important matters, making me feel like an intruder. I didn't like to look at Vida's sister. She looked like a Vida who had been left out in the elements for too long: skin stuck to the bones. Vida did not like her family either. When I asked, she said that her mother was dead and that she did not want to speak of the past. Vida thought of only the future.

Once, when we were alone in her apartment, she asked me if I wanted to see her in a bathing suit. She went into the bathroom and emerged in a tight red one-piece suit. She reclined on the bed in a pose she had obviously seen in a magazine. "Do you think I am beautiful?" she asked me. I answered yes, suddenly overwhelmed by a feeling of hopelessness for my skinny body, bony arms and legs, flat chest. "Cadaverous," Vida had once whispered, smiling wickedly into my face after taking my head into her hands and feeling my skull so close to the surface. But right afterwards she had kissed my cheek, reassuring me that I would "flesh out" in a few years.

That summer my life shifted on its axis. Until Vida, my mother had been the magnetic force around which all my actions revolved. Since my father was away for long periods of time, my young mother and I had developed a strong symbiotic relationship, with me playing the part of interpreter and buffer to the world for her. I knew at an early age that I would be the one to face landlords, doctors, store clerks, and other "strangers" whose services we needed in my father's absence. English was my weapon and my power. As long as she lived in her fantasy that her exile from Puerto Rico was temporary and that she did not need to learn the language, keeping herself "pure" for her return to the island, then I was in control of our lives outside the realm of our little apartment in Paterson—that is, until Father came home from his Navy tours: Then the mantle of responsibility would fall on him. At times, I resented his homecomings, when I would suddenly be thrust back into the role of dependent which I had long ago outgrown—and not by choice.

But Vida changed me. I became secretive, and every outing from our apartment building—to get my mother a pack of L&Ms; to buy essentials at the drugstore or supermarket (which my mother liked to do on an as-needed basis); and, Vida's favorite, to buy Puerto Rican groceries at the bodega—became an adventure with Vida. She was getting restless living in such close quarters with her paranoid sister and brother-in-law. The baby's crying and the pervasive smells of dirty diapers drove her crazy, as did her fat grandmother's lethargy, which was disturbed only by the old woman's need to lecture Vida about her style of dress and her manners, which even my mother had started to comment on.

Vida was modeling herself on the go-go girls she loved to watch on dance shows on our television set. She would imitate their movements with me as her audience until we both fell on the sofa laughing. Her eye make-up (bought with my allowance) was dark and heavy, her lips were glossy with iridescent tan lipstick, and her skirts were riding higher and higher on her long legs. When we walked up the street on one of my errands, the men stared; the Puerto Rican men did more than that. More than once we were followed by men inspired to compose *piropos* for Vida—erotically charged words spoken behind us in stage whispers.

I was scared and excited by the trail of Vida's admirers. It was a dangerous game for both of us, but for me especially, since my father could come home unannounced at any time and catch me at it. I was the invisible partner in Vida's life; I was her little pocket mirror she could take out any time to confirm her beauty and her power. But I was too young to think in those terms; all I knew was the thrill of being in her company, being touched by her magical powers of transformation that could make a walk to the store a deliciously sinful escapade.

Then Vida fell in love. He was, in my jealous eyes, a Neanderthal, a big hairy man who drove a large black Oldsmobile recklessly around our block hour after hour just to catch a glimpse of Vida. He had promised to drive her to California, she confided to me. Then she started to use me as cover in order to meet him, asking me to take a walk with her, then leaving me to wait on a park bench or at the library for what seemed an eternity while she drove around with her muscle-bound lover. I became disenchanted with Vida, but remained loyal to her throughout the summer. Once in a while we still shared a good time. She loved to tell me in detail about her "romance." Apparently, she was not totally naive, and had managed to keep their passionate encounters within the limits of kissing and petting in the spacious backseat of the black Oldsmobile. But he was getting impatient, she told me, so she had decided to announce her engagement to her family soon. They would get married and go to California together. He would be her manager and protect her from the Hollywood "wolves."

By this time I was getting weary of Vida's illusions about Hollywood. I was glad when school started in the fall and I got into my starched blue jumper only to discover that it was too tight and too short for me. I had "developed" over the summer.

Life settled to our normal routine when we were in the States. This was: My brother and I went to Catholic school and did our lessons, our mother waited for our father to come home on leave from his Navy tours, and all of us waited to hear when we would be returning to Puerto Rico—which was usually every time Father went to Europe, every six months or so. Vida would sometimes come down to our apartment and complain bitterly about life with her family upstairs. They had absolutely refused to accept her fiancé. They were making plans to migrate elsewhere. She did not have work papers yet, but did not want to go with them. She would have to find a place to stay until she got married. She began courting my mother. I would come home to find them looking at bride magazines and laughing together. Vida hardly spoke to me at all.

Father came home in his winter blues and everything changed for us. I felt the almost physical release of the burden of responsibility for my family and allowed myself to spend more time doing what I liked to do best of all—read. It was a solitary life we led in Paterson, New Jersey, and both my brother and I became avid readers. My mother did too, although because she had little English, her fare was made up of Corín Tellado romances, which Schulze's drugstore carried, and the *Buenhogar* and *Vanidades* magazines that she received in the mail occasionally. But she read less and I more when Father came home. The ebb and flow of this routine was interrupted by Vida that year. With my mother's help she introduced herself into our family.

Father, normally a reticent man, suspicious of strangers by nature, and always vigilant about dangers to his children, also fell under Vida's spell. Amazingly, he agreed to let her come stay in our apartment until her wedding some months away. She moved into my room. She slept on what had been my little brother's twin bed until he got his own room, a place where I liked to keep my collection of dolls from around the world that my father had sent me. These had to be put in a box in the dark closet now.

Vida's perfume took over my room. As soon as I walked in, I smelled her. It got on my clothes. The nuns at my school commented on it since we were not allowed to use perfume or cosmetics. I tried to wash it off, but it was strong and pervasive. Vida tried to win me by taking me shopping. She was getting money from her boyfriend—for her trousseau—she said. She bought me a tight black skirt just like hers and a pair of shoes with heels. When she had me model it for my family, my father frowned and left the room silently. I was not allowed to keep these things. Since the man was never seen at our house, we did not know that Vida had broken the engagement and was seeing other men.

My mother started to complain about little things Vida did, or did not do. She did not help with housework, although she did contribute money. Where was she getting it? She did not bathe daily (a major infraction in my mother's eyes), but poured cologne over herself in quantities. She claimed to be at church too many times a week and came home smelling of alcohol, even though it was hard to tell because of the perfume. Mother was spreading her wings and getting ready to fight for exclusivity over her nest.

But, Father, surprising us all again, argued for fairness for the *señorita*. My mother made a funny "harrump" noise at that word, which in Spanish connotes virginity and purity. He said we had promised her asylum until she got settled and it was important that we send her out of our house in a respectable manner: married, if possible. He liked playing cards with her. She was cunning and smart, a worthy adversary.

Mother fumed. My brother and I spent a lot of time in the kitchen or living room, reading where the air was not saturated with "Evening in Paris."

Vida was changing. After a few months, she no longer spoke of Hollywood; she barely spoke to me at all. She got her papers and got a job in a factory sewing dungarees. Then, almost as suddenly as she had come into my life, she disappeared.

One afternoon I came home to find my mother mopping the floors strenuously with a pine cleaner, giving the apartment the kind of thorough scrubbing usually done as a family effort in the spring. When I went into my room, the dolls were back in their former place on the extra bed. No sign of Vida.

I don't remember discussing her parting much. Although my parents were fair, they did not always feel the need to explain or justify their decisions to us. I have always believed that my mother simply demanded her territory, fearing the growing threat of Vida's beauty and erotic slovenliness that was permeating her clean home. Or perhaps Vida found life with us as stifling as she had with her family. If I had been a little older, I would have learned more from Vida, but she came at a time when I needed security more than knowledge of human nature. She was a fascinating creature.

The last time I saw Vida's face it was on a poster. It announced her crowning as a beauty queen for a Catholic church in another parish. Beauty contests were held by churches as fundraisers at that time, as contradictory as that seems to me now: a church sponsoring a competition to choose the most physically attractive female in the congregation. I still feel that it was right to see Vida wearing the little tiara of fake diamonds in that photograph with the caption underneath: Vida wins!

Fulana

She was the woman with no name. The blank filled in
with Fulana in the presence of children.
But we knew her—she was the wild girl
we were not allowed to play with,
who painted her face with her absent mother's make-up,
and who always wanted to be "wife"
when we played house. She was bored
with other games, preferred to turn the radio loud
to songs about women and men
loving and fighting to guitar, maracas, and drums.
She wanted to be a dancer on the stage,
dressed in nothing but yellow feathers.

And she would grow up careless as a bird,
losing contact with her name during the years
when her body was light enough to fly.
But when gravity began to pull her down
to where the land animals chewed the cud
of domestic routine, she was a different
species. She had become Fulana, the creature
bearing the jagged scars of wings on her back,
whose name should not be mentioned
in the presence of impressionable little girls
who might begin to wonder about flight,
how the houses of their earth-bound mothers,
the fields and rivers, and the schools and churches
would look from above.

Kennedy in the Barrio

My sixth-grade class had been assigned to watch the Kennedy inauguration on television, and I did, at the counter of Puerto Habana, the restaurant where my father worked. I heard the Cuban owner Larry Reyes say that an Irish Catholic being elected meant that someday an *hispano* could be president of the United States, too. I saw my father nod in automatic agreement with his boss, but his eyes were not on the grainy screen; he was concerned with the food cooking in the back and with the listless waitress mopping the floor. Larry Reyes turned his attention to me then and raised his cup as if to make a toast: "Here's to a *puertorriqueño* or *puertorriqueña* president of the United States," he laughed, not kindly, I thought. "Right, Elenita?"

I shrugged my shoulders. Later my father would once again reprimand me for not showing Mr. Reyes the proper amount of respect.

Two years and ten months later, I would run to Puerto Habana on a cold Friday afternoon to find a crowd around the television set. Many of them, men and women alike, were sobbing like children. *"Dios mío, Dios mío,"* they kept wailing. A group of huddling women tried to embrace me as I made my way to my parents, who were holding each other tightly, apart from the others. I slipped in between them. I smelled her scent of castile soap, *café con leche* and cinnamon; I inhaled his mixture of sweat and Old Spice cologne—a man-smell that I was afraid to like too much.

That night at Puerto Habana Larry Reyes and my father served free food. Both of them wore black armbands. My mother cooked and I bused tables. An old woman started reciting the rosary aloud, and soon practically everyone was kneeling on that hard linoleum floor, praying and sobbing for our dead president. Exhausted from the outpouring of public grief and exasperated by the displays of uncontrolled emotion I had witnessed that day, the *ay benditos*, the kisses and embraces of strangers I had had to endure, I asked if I could go home early. For the first time, my vigilant mother trusted me to walk alone at night without the usual lecture about the dangers of the streets. The dark, empty silence of our apartment gave me no solace, and in a turmoil of emotions I had never experienced before, I went to sleep the night of the day President Kennedy died. I rose the next day to a world that looked the same.

*L*ost *Relatives*

In the great diaspora
of our chromosomes,
we've lost track of one another.
Living our separate lives,
unaware of the alliance of our flesh,
we have at times recognized
our kinship through the printed word:
Classifieds, where we trade our lives
in two-inch columns;
Personals, straining our bloodlines
with our lonely hearts; and
Obituaries, announcing a vacancy
in our family history
through names that call us home
with their familiar syllables.

Gravity

My bedroom was my inner sanctum where I kept my books, my radio—which was always on when I was there—and the other symbols of my rebellion: tie-dye t-shirts, Indian headbands and jewelry that made music when I moved; a stick of patchouli incense burning on its wooden stand. My mother decorated the rest of the place in what I referred to as Early Puerto Rican: a religious print in every room. I had removed my Guardian Angel from my wall, the one depicting a winged creature in flowing robes leading a little girl and boy over the rickety bridge. (The children appeared to be as oblivious to their guardian as to the dark abyss opening up beneath them.) I was taking a stand by refusing to decorate with angels and saints, and by disdaining everything my parents loved. My mother put the picture up in the hallway, right in front of my bedroom door so that I'd have to see it coming in and out. It came to be a symbol for me of our relationship in those days.

Evenings she'd sit in her rocking chair in the living room and listen to record albums she bought on the Island during our yearly visits to her mother's home: Celia Cruz, Felipe Rodríguez, and the big band music of Tito Puente, which she played loud to compete with my Little Richard, the Supremes, Dylan and, later, the Beatles, the Beatles, the Beatles. When my father came home we both turned down the volume. He had to listen to the *vellonera*, a monstrous juke-box going all day long at the restaurant where he worked for the "magnanimous" Mr. Larry Reyes. My mother and father thought everything he did was inspired, including naming the place Puerto Habana to please both his Puerto Rican and Cuban clientele. Papi had to endure listening to the same popular records played over and over by the regulars. When he came home he expected two things: that the music be kept down and that we all sit down to dinner together.

It was my clothes that visibly upset him. He could not keep himself from staring at my waist-long hair worn loose and wild but encircled, for decoration, by a headband embroidered in Navajo designs. I also wore bell-bottom blue jeans torn and faded just right, and the orange sunburst tie-dye t-shirts, once his undershirts, in fact, which I had borrowed from the clothesline to experiment with. This is how I was dressed on New Year's Eve, 1965. In my room, Dylan's "The Times They Are A-Changin'" was playing softly on the radio.

I knew that my rebel disguise worried my parents, but we had an unspoken agreement we all understood would be revoked if they objected too much to my hippie clothes and loud music. By day I looked and acted like a good Catholic girl, wearing my Queen of Heaven High School uniform of gray plaid wool, penny-loafers with socks, hair in a braid, the whole bit. After school I became whoever and whatever I wanted.

I felt that the sacrifice of my ideals for eight hours was worth it to be around Sister Mary Joseph, the counter-culture nun who fed us revolutionary literature and Eastern philosophy under the guise of teaching English literature. I was getting an excellent education at the Catholic school although I felt no more a part of the mostly Irish student body than I had at Public School Number 16 in my barrio, among "my own kind." But at Queen of Heaven I was at least free from barrio pressures, even if never asked to join the sororities or invited to parties. And even this was changing as the *Movement* infected the clean-cut crowds. Sister Mary Joseph had started a café in an unused basement room where on Fridays, four or five of us *hairier* students met with her to listen to the exotic records she brought—music to feed our souls: Gregorian chants, Tibetan drums and bells, poets reading their doomsday verses in funereal tones to the rhythms of lyres. We sat in the lotus position and meditated or talked excitedly about "the Revolution."

I had fallen for one of the boys, a tall, thin, black-haired nascent poet named Gerald who wore a purple beret that matched the dark circles under his eyes. He looked like my idea of a poet. He would later become known in our crowd for being the only one among us to go to Woodstock. The *trip* would cost him: LSD would leave him so disconnected that he would have to spend six months in a "home." But the aura of the "event" he would bring back was perhaps worth the high price to Gerald—we'd remember him as the only one among us who witnessed the phenomenon of Woodstock firsthand. But that was still years away. When I had my crush on him, Gerald's rebellion was still in its pupa stage. At school we shared our poems and fueled each other's intensity.

Our café was at first scorned by the other kids. Then, perhaps because our little group was self-sufficient, even the popular kids asked about what we did in the basement and wanted to be taken there. Once we opened it up to the "others," the club lost some of its intimacy and mystery, but it widened the circle of my social life too.

I could never ask any of my friends over to our apartment. They would have suffered culture shock. So I divided myself into two people—actually three, if you counted the after-school hippie version as a separate identity. It was not always easy to shuffle out of my visionary self and into the binding coat of propriety the Puerto Rican girl was supposed to wear, although my parents were more understanding than others in our barrio.

That New Year's Eve, we were supposed to attend the annual party at the restaurant, Puerto Habana. That meant my father would be stuck behind the bar serving Budweisers and rum-and-cokes all night. My mother would play hostess for the owner, Mr. Reyes, who would be busy accepting everyone's gratitude and good wishes. I knew I was not dressed appropriately for the occasion, but I was looking to expand my horizons in the new year with a few new brazen acts of rebellion.

"Elenita," my mother began as she cleared the table, "did you forget about the fiesta tonight?"

"No, María Elena, I did not forget about the fiesta tonight." (I had also decided to call my mother by her first name as an experiment in "evolving" our roles.)

She frowned at me, but said nothing about it. I suspected that she and my father had "strategized" about how best to handle me. "Just ignore her. It's a stage. It will pass, you'll see," I could just hear them saying to each other.

"Then why are you not dressed?"

"I am dressed, María Elena. I'm not naked, am I?"

"How about that pretty green taffeta dress we bought you for Honors Day?"

That horrible mistake of a dress was in the back of my closet. My mother had insisted we buy it when I had won a certificate for an essay I had written in English class: "Brave New World For Women." Sister Mary Joseph had been one of the judges. My mother had bought me a party dress to wear to school that day. I had worn it into the girls' lavatory, where I had promptly changed to a plain black skirt and white blouse.

"It's too small for me now. Maybe you haven't noticed but I have breasts now."

She dropped a tin pot noisily into the sink and faced me. I had said *breasts* in front of my father. She knew I was deliberately provoking her.

He, in the meantime, had gulped down the last of his coffee and hurriedly kissed her cheek, exiting. "I'll be waiting for you at Puerto, *querida*. I promised *el Señor* Reyes I would open early. Please be careful walking there. The sidewalks are icy," he said, without looking at me. He knew how I felt about his boss, the imperialist Lorenzo, *alias* Larry, Reyes.

For the greater part of my childhood I had practically lived with my parents at Puerto Habana. My father opened and closed the restaurant: twelve-hour days. And my mother was always on stand-by, as cook, waitress, hostess, whatever Reyes needed; and almost every day, she was needed. My father thought of the restaurant as the heart of his barrio life. On the other hand, Mami talked constantly about the family on the Island. It was point-counterpoint every day, not quite an argument, just an ongoing discussion about where "home" was for each of them.

Papi's reasons for not going back to Puerto Rico with us varied from year to year: Not the right time, not enough money, he was needed here by Mr. Reyes. It was only years later that I learned through my mother's stories that Jorge was ashamed of the fact that he could not provide for us the kinds of luxuries my mother had had growing up in a middle-class family in Puerto Rico. He felt rejected by her mother and scorned by his successful brother-in-law. His—our— lower middle-class status, actually more like middle working-class level, did not bother him any other time, however. When he talked about Puerto Habana, his job there which allowed him contact with just about everyone in our barrio, he sounded proud. Every other sentence began with his benefactor's name, Larry Reyes. Larry Reyes plans to open the restaurant after regular hours to serve a special free meal *para los mayores,* for the old people. Larry Reyes is sending baskets to the sick ones who cannot come to Puerto Habana. Every week Larry Reyes had a new scheme which my father committed himself to, heart and soul, and his free time. He would be there to serve the old people after regular hours. And he and Mother would get his old black Buick out of its parking spot in the back of the restaurant and ride to decrepit places all over town delivering sandwiches and hot *asopao,* chicken soup Puerto Rican style, in thermos jugs to everyone on Reyes's list.

Sometimes I would go with them and sit in the cold car rather than go into dark hallways that smelled of urine and other unimaginable human waste and decay. My mother often came out with tears in her eyes. On the way home she would tell us stories of how she and her mother had also delivered food and medicines in Puerto Rico during the war: "But it was never like this, Jorge. The poor on the island did not live in this kind of filth. There was the river to bathe in, if there was no plumbing. There was a garden to grow a few things. They would not starve as long as they had a little plot of earth. Jorge, this is not living!" And she would sob a little. His arm would be around her shoulders. He would kiss her on the forehead and talk about how good it was to be able to help people, even in a small way.

Yeah, right, I'd be thinking, huddled in the back seat, the poor people of her dream island didn't have the swollen bellies of malnutrion I had read about in books, nor did they have to drink the putrid waters of rivers now polluted with human and industrial waste in the famous slums of her island paradise. My irritation at my parents' naiveté grew along with my suspicion of Reyes's acts of charity.

Reyes was an easier target for my self-righteous anger than my parents, whom I saw as victims of his schemes. I believed that he was doing these things for himself: He saw himself as the Don in our barrio, the businessman-philanthropist. Yet he never got his hands dirty dealing with the poor. It was always my mother's heart that broke, and my father's back. And our family time that was usurped. I resolved to get out of this system of haves, have-nots and in-betweens that dominated our lives in the barrio. I learned about the feudal system of king, lords and peasants in my history class, and I thought I saw a clear analogy between the barrio structure and the Middle Ages. I would not be trapped in this web of deceit with the capitalist Reyes as the fat spider in the middle.

Since I didn't even have a driver's license yet, my revolt was at that time limited to small acts of defiance, like the one I had planned to execute that New Year's Eve, to let at least my mother know where I stood.

"Elena. Why are you so fresh? If you are a *señorita* as you are always telling me, why don't you act like one?"

But it was she who was always reminding me to act like a *señorita,* which meant the opposite to her of what *I* thought. I felt I was an adult, or at least on the verge. To her it meant that I was to act more *decente:* Sit right so that your underwear doesn't show under your mini-skirt, do not mention sex or body parts in front of men—not even your own father—don't do this, don't do that. To me being fifteen meant that I should be allowed at least to choose my own clothes, my own friends, and to say whatever I wanted to say when I wanted to say it—free country, right?

"Maybe I won't go to this party." I had no wish to socialize with the barrio's matrons and their over-dressed daughters, nor to dance with older men, including Reyes, whose breath stank of rum and cigarettes and who would be crying like babies at the stroke of midnight, *"¡Ay mi Cuba! ¡Ay mi Borinquén!"* All calling out for their islands, and shedding tears for their old *mamás* who waited in their *casas* for their *hijos* to come home. Actually, though I would never have admitted it then, I loved the dancing and the food, and especially listening to the women tell dirty jokes at their tables while the men played dominoes and got drunk at theirs. But I had taken my battle position.

"Está bien, hija."

She caught me totally by surprise when she said in a sad, resigned voice that I could do as I wished.

"You are old enough to stay here alone. I have to help Jorge." She left me at the kitchen table, defeated by her humble acceptance of my decision when I had hoped for a little fight—one that I could have graciously finally lost—though I was firm on the matter of the puke-green taffeta dress.

Minutes later she emerged from her room looking like a Mexican movie star. She wore a tight-fitting black satin dress with a low neck, showing off her impressive bosom—which made me ashamed to have brought up the subject of my negligible little buds. She had her hair up in a French twist to show off the cameo earrings her Jorge had given her for Christmas. María Elena was still a beautiful woman—though hopelessly behind the times.

"Lock the door behind me, will you, Elenita," she said, her voice soft and sad. I nodded as she walked away without a glance back at me.

An hour or so later I found myself looking through my closet for a reasonable compromise between taffeta and denim.

As always on New Year's Eve, my father asked me to dance the last dance of the year with him, and at midnight he held my mother as she wept in his arms for her *isla* and her *familia* so far away. This time I did not just feel my usual little pang of jealousy for being left out of their perceptions. Seeing the way she held on to him, and how he placed his lips on her tear-streaked face as if to absorb her grief, I felt a need awakening in me, a sort of hunger to connect with someone of my own. One minute into the new year—the beginning of the year of my revolution—and it had nothing to do with the times, but with time's only gift to us: the love that binds us, its gravitational pull.

They Say

They say
when I arrived,
traveling light,
the women who waited
plugged
the cracks in the walls
with rags
dipped in alcohol
to keep drafts and demons out.
Candles were lit
to the Virgen.
They say
Mother's breath
kept blowing them out
right and left.
When I slipped
into their hands
the room was in shadows.
They say
I nearly turned away,
undoing
the hasty knot of my umbilicus.
They say
my urge to bleed
told them I was like a balloon
with a leak,

a soul trying to fly away
through the cracks in the wall.
The midwife sewed
and the women prayed
as they fitted
me for life
in a tight corset of gauze.
But their prayers held me back,
the bandages held me in,
and all that night
they dipped
their bloody rags.
They say
Mother slept through it all,
blowing out
candles
with her breath.

amacita

Mamacita hummed all day long
over the caboose kitchen
of our railroad flat.
From my room I'd hear her *humm*,
No words slowed the flow
of Mamacita's soulful sounds;
it was *humm* over the yellow rice,
and *umm* over the black beans.
Up and down two syllables she'd climb
and slide—each note a task accomplished.
From chore to chore, she was the prima donna
in her daily operetta.
Mamacita's wordless song was her connection
to the oversoul,
her link with life,
her mantra,
a lifeline to her own Laughing Buddha,
as she dragged her broom
across a lifetime of linoleum floors.

First Love

At fourteen and for a few years after, my concerns were focused mainly on the alarms going off in my body warning me of pain or pleasure ahead.

I fell in love, or my hormones awakened from their long slumber in my body, and suddenly the goal of my days was focused on one thing: to catch a glimpse of my secret love. And it had to remain secret, because I had, of course, in the great tradition of tragic romance, chosen to love a boy who was totally out of my reach. He was not Puerto Rican; he was Italian and rich. He was also an older man. He was a senior at the high school when I came in as a freshman. I first saw him in the hall, leaning casually on a wall that was the border line between girlside and boyside for under-classmen. He looked extraordinarily like a young Marlon Brando—down to the ironic little smile. The total of what I knew about the boy who starred in every one of my awkward fantasies was this: He was the nephew of the man who owned the supermarket on my block; he often had parties at his parents' beau-tiful home in the suburbs which I would hear about; this family had money (which came to our school in many ways)—and this last fact made my knees weak: He worked at the store near my apartment building on weekends and in the summer.

My mother could not understand why I became so eager to be the one sent out on her endless errands. I pounced on every opportunity from Friday to late

Saturday afternoon to go after eggs, cigarettes, milk (I tried to drink as much of it as possible, although I hated the stuff)—the staple items that she would order from the "American" store.

Week after week I wandered up and down the aisles, taking furtive glances at the stock room in the back, breathlessly hoping to see my prince. Not that I had a plan. I felt like a pilgrim waiting for a glimpse of Mecca. I did not expect him to notice me. It was sweet agony.

One day I did see him. Dressed in a white outfit like a surgeon; white pants and shirt, white cap, and (gross sight, but not to my love-glazed eyes) blood-smeared butcher's apron. He was helping to drag a side of beef into the freezer storage area of the store. I must have stood there like an idiot, because I remember that he did see me, he even spoke to me! I could have died. I think he said, "Excuse me," and smiled vaguely in my direction.

After that, I willed occasions to go to the supermarket. I watched my mother's pack of cigarettes empty ever so slowly. I wanted her to smoke them fast. I drank milk and forced it on my brother (although a second glass for him had to be bought with my share of Fig Newton cookies, which we both liked, but we were restricted to one row each). I gave my cookies up for love, and watched my mother smoke her L&Ms with so little enthusiasm that I thought (God, no!) that she might be cutting down on her smoking or maybe even giving up the habit. At this crucial time!

I thought I had kept my lonely romance a secret. Often I cried hot tears on my pillow for the things that kept us apart. In my mind there was no doubt that he would never notice me (and that is why I felt free to stare at him—I was invisible). He could not see me because I was a skinny Puerto Rican girl, a freshman who did not belong to any group he associated with.

At the end of the year I found out that I had not been invisible. I learned one little lesson about human nature—adulation leaves a scent, one that we are all equipped to recognize, and no matter how insignificant the source, we seek it.

Each June, the nuns at our school would always arrange for some cultural extravaganza. In my freshman year it was a Roman banquet. We had been studying Greek drama (as a prelude to church history—it was at a fast clip that we galloped through Sophocles and Euripides toward the early Christian martyrs), and our young, energetic Sister Agnes was in the mood for spectacle. She ordered the entire student body (a small group of under 300 students) to have our mothers make us togas out of sheets. She handed out a pattern on mimeo pages fresh out of the machine. I remember the intense smell of the alcohol on the sheets of paper, and how almost everyone in the auditorium brought theirs to their noses and inhaled deeply—mimeographed handouts were the school-day buzz that the new Xerox generation of kids is missing out on. Then, as the last couple of weeks of school dragged on, the city of Paterson becoming a concrete oven, and us wilting in our uncomfortable uniforms, we labored like frantic Roman slaves to build a splendid banquet hall in our small auditorium.

Sister Agnes wanted a raised dais where the host and hostess would be regally enthroned.

She had already chosen our Senator and Lady from among our ranks. The Lady was to be a beautiful new student named Sophia, a recent Polish immigrant, whose English was still practically unintelligible, but whose features, classically perfect without a trace of makeup, enthralled us. Everyone talked about her gold hair cascading past her waist, and her voice which could carry a note right up to heaven in choir. The nuns wanted her for God. They kept saying that she had a vocation. We just looked at her in awe, and the boys seemed afraid of her. She just smiled and did as she was told. I don't know what she thought of it all. The main privilege of beauty is that others will do almost everything for you, including thinking.

Her partner was to be our best basketball player, a tall, red-haired senior whose family sent its many offspring to our school. Together, Sophia and her senator looked like the best combination of immigrant genes our community could produce. It did not occur to me to ask then whether anything but their physical beauty qualified them for the starring roles in our production. I had the highest average in the church history class, but I was given the part of one of many "Roman citizens." I was to sit in front of the plastic fruit and recite a greeting in Latin along with the rest of the school when our hosts came into the hall and took their places on their throne.

On the night of our banquet, my father escorted me in my toga to the door of our school. I felt foolish in my awkwardly draped sheet (blouse and skirt required underneath). My mother had no great skill as a seamstress. The best she could do was hem a skirt or a pair of pants. That night I would have traded her for a peasant woman with a golden needle. I saw other Roman ladies emerging from their parents' cars looking authentic in sheets of material that folded over their bodies like the garments on a statue by Michelangelo. How did they do it? How was it that I always got it just slightly wrong? And worse, I believed that other people were just too polite to mention it. "The poor little Puerto Rican girl," I could hear them thinking. But in reality, I must have been my worst critic, self-conscious as I was.

Soon, we were all sitting at our circle of tables joined together around the dais. Sophia glittered like a golden statue. Her smile was beatific: a perfect, silent Roman lady. Her "senator" looked uncomfortable, glancing around at his buddies, perhaps waiting for the ridicule that he would surely get in the locker room later. The nuns in their black habits stood in the background watching us. What were they supposed to be, the Fates? Nubian slaves? The dancing girls did their modest little dance to tinny music from their finger cymbals, then the speeches were made. Then the grape vine "wine" was raised in a toast to the Roman Empire we all knew would fall within the week—before finals anyway.

All during the program I had been in a state of controlled hysteria. My secret love sat across the room from me looking supremely bored. I watched his every move, taking him in gluttonously. I relished the shadow of his eyelashes on his ruddy cheeks, his pouty lips smirking sarcastically at the ridiculous sight of our little play. Once he slumped down on his chair, and our sergeant-at-arms nun came over and tapped him sharply on his shoulder. He drew himself up slowly, with disdain. I loved his rebellious spirit. I believed myself still invisible to him in my "nothing" status as I looked upon my beloved. But towards the end of the evening, as we stood chanting our farewells in Latin, he looked straight across the room and into my eyes! How did I survive the killing power of those dark pupils? I trembled in a new way. I was not cold—I was burning! Yet I shook from the inside out, feeling light-headed, dizzy.

The room began to empty and I headed for the girls' lavatory. I wanted to relish the miracle in silence. I did not think for a minute that anything more would follow. I was satisfied with the enormous favor of a look from my beloved. I took my time, knowing that my father would be waiting outside for me, impatient, perhaps glowing in the dark in his phosphorescent white Navy uniform. The others would ride home. I would walk home with my father, both of us in costume. I wanted as few witnesses as possible. When I could no longer hear the crowds in the hallway, I emerged from the bathroom, still under the spell of those mesmerizing eyes.

The lights had been turned off in the hallway and all I could see was the lighted stairwell, at the bottom of which a nun would be stationed. My father would be waiting just outside. I nearly screamed when I felt someone grab me by the waist. But my mouth was quickly covered by someone else's mouth. I was being kissed. My first kiss and I could not even tell who it was. I pulled away to see that face not two inches away from mine. It was he. He smiled down at me. Did I have a silly expression on my face? My glasses felt crooked on my nose. I was unable to move or to speak. More gently, he lifted my chin and touched his lips to mine. This time I did not forget to enjoy it. Then, like the phantom lover that he was, he walked away into the darkened corridor and disappeared.

I don't know how long I stood there. My body was changing right there in the hallway of a Catholic school. My cells were tuning up like musicians in an orchestra, and my heart was a chorus. It was an opera I was composing, and I wanted to stand very still and just listen. But, of course, I heard my father's voice talking to the nun. I was in trouble if he had had to ask about me. I hurried down the stairs making up a story on the way about feeling sick. That would explain my flushed face and it would buy me a little privacy when I got home.

The next day Father announced at the breakfast table that he was leaving on a six-month tour of Europe with the Navy in a few weeks and, that at the end of the school year my mother, my brother, and I would be sent to Puerto Rico to stay for half a year at Mama's (my maternal grandmother's) house. I was devastated. This was the usual routine for us. We had always gone to Mama's to stay when Father was away for long periods. But this year it was different for me. I was in love, and . . . my heart knocked against my bony chest at this thought . . . he loved me too? I broke into sobs and left the table.

In the next week I discovered the inexorable truth about parents. They can actually carry on with their plans right through tears, threats, and the awful spectacle of a teenager's broken heart. My father left me to my mother, who impassively packed while I explained over and over that I was at a crucial time in my studies and that if I left my entire life would be ruined. All she would say is, "You are an intelligent girl, you'll catch up." Her head was filled with visions of *casa* and family reunions, long gossip sessions with her mama and sisters. What did she care that I was losing my one chance at true love?

In the meantime I tried desperately to see him. I thought he would look for me too. But the few times I saw him in the hallway, he was always rushing away. It would be long weeks of confusion and pain before I realized that the kiss was nothing but a little trophy for his ego. He had no interest in me other than as his adorer. He was flattered by my silent worship of him, and he had bestowed a kiss on me to please himself, and to fan the flames. I learned a lesson about the battle of the sexes then that I have never forgotten: The object is not always to win, but most times simply to keep your opponent (synonymous at times with "the loved one") guessing.

But this is too cynical a view to sustain in the face of that overwhelming rush of emotion that is first love. And in thinking back about my own experience with it, I can be objective only to the point where I recall how sweet the anguish was, how caught up in the moment I felt, and how every nerve in my body was involved in this salute to life.

Judith Ortiz Cofer
–62–

Later, much later, after what seemed like an eternity of dragging the weight of unrequited love around with me, I learned to make myself visible and to relish the little battles required to win the greatest prize of all. And much later, I read and understood Albert Camus's statement about the subject that concerns both adolescent and philosopher alike: If love were easy, life would be too simple.

$\mathcal{M}$aking $\mathcal{L}$ove in Spanish, circa 1969

It was my summer of mourning and tears. And it was my grandmother, Mamá María, who changed the ordinary course of my life. She sent me to return a borrowed serving dish to her neighbor one day during the summer I spent with her in Puerto Rico after the death of Papá José. It was there that I met Pito, the soldier-boy, convalescing at home after having been wounded almost immediately upon arriving in Vietnam. I had heard a woman in the *pueblo* call him "damaged goods." When I came upon him that sweltering June day, he was coiled in his nest of pain and anger on his mother's sofa. He saw me first and lifted his head up on one elbow, narrowing his eyes as if the light I had let in had blinded him.

"Good afternoon, Miss Niña," he said in English. I was startled by the deep voice coming from the shadows in an airless room where all the windows were shut. Mamá María had instructed me not to knock, just go into the house and find the half-deaf Doña Bárbara in her bedroom, where she sewed for hours most days. Caught by surprise, I stood there with a dish in my hands as the thin wiry man in fatigues swung his feet to the floor and sat straight up in one motion. His head was shaved, and his skull was a shade lighter than his face, which gave him a bizarre, divided look. He kept smiling at me, and I noticed how big and white his teeth looked against his deeply tanned face. His huge liquid eyes were his most stunning feature, however. They seemed unnaturally brilliant and dilated, making me feel frozen to the spot like an animal facing oncoming headlights. Finally I managed a hesitant "hello" and stupidly offered him the dish in my hands.

"*¿Hablas inglés?*" he asked, still grinning, ignoring the dish in my visibly trembling hands. I nodded, looking back at the sliver of light coming through the front door, planning my escape route.

"Then let's talk in English. I have to practice since I am going back to *los Estados Unidos* soon." He winked at me. Then he took the dish, grabbing my hand along with it. He led me to the kitchen, where he stood at the sink and methodically rinsed and dried the dish. Afterwards, he opened one cabinet door after another as if looking for exactly the right spot for it. When every shelf and cupboard had been inspected, he sighed and laid the plate down on the counter.

"It is true, you know, what my sergeant kept saying to me in the Army: Spics just ain't organized; that's why we'll never amount to anything in the world. This island will never be a world power, *niña*, because my mother is totally disorganized. Don't get me wrong, I love my *Mamá*, but she believes the Virgin Mary will help her find something when she needs it. Is your *Mamá* like that? If we have no political future, it's because our mothers do not comprehend the basic concept of organization. Do you agree?"

Stunned by the strange barrage of words, I just nodded. I let him lead me around the dark, empty house, fascinated by his rambling speech and dramatic manner. I had never met anyone like him. It was as if he were performing and I had somehow wandered upon the stage and been incorporated into the act. In a lethargy, caused perhaps by the heat or by the promise of a more interesting day than I had been having at my grandmother's, I played passively along.

As we walked around the old house hand in hand, he talked non-stop in both Spanish and English. His mother's old-fashioned pedal sewing machine had been abandoned for the day, he explained to me, because she had to go to a wake. "She went to watch a dead woman. Why? Where is a woman, who was not allowed out of the house during her lifetime, going to go now that she is dead?"

I was bombarded with, but not given time to answer, many questions that were peculiar but interesting to me since they reflected my own curiosity about the lives of people in a country I had left as a child. He brought us to an abrupt stop at the bathroom door. I must have looked somewhat taken aback, because he smiled and made a military-style about-face before he went in, though he left the door wide open. I just stood there watching him from behind, not knowing what to expect, but fascinated by this boy who couldn't be more than twenty or twenty-one but had already been shot and had maybe even killed people. Through a sweaty t-shirt clinging to his skin, I could tell he had the body of a swimmer, wide shoulders tapering down to a small waist, and his movements were like a syncopated dance, both militarily crisp and graceful. He was still talking as he turned the faucets on full blast.

"They call me Pito here, in that quaint way PRs have of giving you nicknames out of love or spite," he said as he scrubbed his hands under the water, like a surgeon about to operate, soaping all the way to the elbow. After drying his hands and arms with a white towel inscribed with a row of numbers, he again about-faced and saluted me.

"My real name is Angel José Montalvo Matos, your servant." He bowed, reaching for my hands and kissing them. He closed the bathroom door behind him as if suddenly aware of having worried me.

"I had to cleanse myself first, *niña,*" he explained in a hurt tone, "before touching you."

I shook my head in disbelief. By then I was beginning to feel a little anxious at his erratic behavior and odd words. But I was also excited by him and curious.

"Tell me, *niña,* are you of legal age to be in a house alone with a war veteran?"

I didn't bother to answer. I knew he wasn't expecting answers from me. Once again he was leading me from room to room, talking non-stop and asking me absurd, unanswerable questions. Finally, we came to what I presumed was his room. The door was closed. Pito put his hands around my waist but kept our bodies firmly apart at arms-length. I could feel a kind of electrical current running down his arms and into his fingers, almost a tremor. He brought his face close to mine without letting our bodies touch. I thought he was going to kiss me. And, suddenly, I wanted him to put his mouth on mine, I needed to feel his electric arms around my body. I closed my eyes, put what I thought was a romantic expression on my face and waited for a movie-style kiss. My first by a man. Nothing happened, although I could feel his warm breath on my cheek. Finally, feeling my face burning in a hot blush of shame, I opened my eyes and met his intense gaze and ironic smile. I tried to get away, embarrassed that he knew I had been expecting to be kissed. I was also a little frightened by the wildness I saw in his eyes, now so close I thought heat was emanating from them. He stared intently at me, as if he were trying to see what I was thinking and feeling. He squeezed my fingers until they hurt and I cried out. I pulled away, now really ready to get away from him. I ran to the front door, where I was momentarily halted by his voice.

"Come back tomorrow when you see me close the windows in the living room. *Mañana, niña,* I will show you things in there."

I knew "there" meant his room, the only space in his house we had not toured. I hurried out into the white heat of the day. I ran all the way to Mamá's porch, where I sat down on the cool tile floor so that he could not see me from his house. *No way,* I told myself, *no way I'll go back there.* The man was obviously crazy.

❧

The way the world has changed for women, Mamá María had said to me after my grandfather's funeral, is that in her mother's time men buried women. Women died in childbirth, or of overwork, or of one of the many diseases that men brought home from their vices and from other women—things that you can get medicine for now. It was not unusual for a man to be widowed two or three times and to father several generations of children. But this had changed. Now women had to learn to live without men, since for the past sixty years men seem to be more determined than ever to kill each other in one war after the next. She herself had lost two brothers in the first world war, a son in the second, and a nephew to Vietnam. I now thought about Doña Bárbara, whose son had come home alive from the war. Did she consider herself one of the lucky ones?

Ꝙ❧

Although I had no intention of seeing the crazy Pito again, the next day I happened to be walking toward the plaza for an ice cream cone when, at the very moment I passed Doña Bárbara's house, the window facing the street was shut hard with a report that echoed like a gunshot at siesta time. What could I have been thinking as my body turned towards the battened-down house, as if I was being compelled by a force greater than my better judgement and free will, hurrying towards what I knew without a doubt was a dangerous situation?

He had seen me coming and had closed all the other windows with the same force, as if providing my feet with a trail of sound to follow. Once inside I saw the beam of yellow light emanating from his room and I traced it there. My heart was pounding so hard that I had trouble breathing. Pito was spread out on

his bed like Christ on the cross, the same calmly ago-
nized expression on his face, wearing nothing but a
cut-off pair of fatigues. A light-bulb hanging from the
ceiling swung like a pendulum over him, and his
pupils moved to follow its arc. As I ran my eyes over
his half-naked body, I saw that running from his navel
down into his pants there was a long scar crookedly
dividing the smooth expanse of his torso.

I became aware that he was watching me examin-
ing him from the corner of his eyes, but he had not
acknowledged my presence. I could have left then, but
my feet did not know exactly what my brain wanted
them to do, since I felt like heading in two directions
simultaneously.

"You may touch it, if you like," he whispered, still
staring at the ceiling. Although I was certain that he
saw me too, perhaps I had started to move away.
Slowly, seductively he traced the scar with his index
finger to the point where it met his waist-band while I
stood frozen at the threshold to his room.

"I think I'd better go," I finally said, not moving.

That's when Pito swung his legs off the bed and
into a standing position in one graceful movement.
He was one inch from me before I had taken another
breath.

"No, *niña,* you must not be afraid of Pito, or of his
ugly wound. It's healed. *Mira.*" He placed my hand on
his stomach and moved it over the tough cord-like surface of the scar. I was practically immobile on the
outside, but I felt ready to disintegrate or perhaps
melt into a puddle right there in front of Pito. I had
never before felt the mixture of horror and attraction

that he was now inspiring in me. Was this desire? I did not know for certain. After guiding my fingers over the raised scar with his own hand, he placed my open palm over his heart. He kept his eyes locked with mine while releasing my hand from his grip slowly and carefully, as if he did not trust me to keep it there on my own.

After some moments of keeping me in this trance of almost touching, he gently led me by the hand to his bed, where he molded my body to his in a total embrace of heads, arms and legs that seemed as perfect and right as the right key fitting in the right lock. He held me so tightly that I had to push away a little to breathe.

"I will not do anything you do not want me to do, *niña*," he spoke with his mouth close to my ear so that his voice seemed to enter my mind like a message in a dream. I felt his lips moving on my skin, forming the words out of the charged air between us. "You tell me what you want me to do and I will do it."

Then he added in a different tone, slightly mocking, "But you must say it in Spanish. I only make love in Spanish. *¿Comprendes?*"

Not knowing what else to do, I nodded.

"Now repeat after me: Kiss me. *Bésame.*"

"*Bésame,*" I said. And he did. He kissed me in my native language until I forgot all others existed.

It was the summer of mourning and tears. When I came home from Pito's bed that day, I thought I had found and lost love in one afternoon. I felt confused about how I felt, and all I knew was that I was sadder than I had ever been in my life. Pito had kissed me until my mouth hurt. He had touched me where I wanted to be touched and he had waited until I asked him to make love to me. And he had tried. It was then, pressing my face to his chest so that I could not look at him, that he had told me I was the first woman he had tried to make love with since his return from Vietnam. He told me that he had refused to believe the American doctors when they had told him about the muscle and nerve damage the landmine had inflicted. It was the same mine that had killed another man, a buddy who marched in front of him, whose body had partially shielded Pito. Pito spoke in a cool detached voice, as if this was a speech he had long prepared to give. He had come home against the their advice, but was considering moving to New York, where he might or might not go through some kind of operation they had told him about.

After he finished talking he held me in his arms for a long while. I tried to comfort him, saying I understood, but I really didn't know how to understand him. This was my first experience dealing with the unimaginable dual forces of death and sex. I wanted to feel sorry for Pito's terrible loss, but instead I felt cheated of the moment I had dreamed of ever since I had first thought of loving a man. And I felt ashamed of my feelings.

Dressing in the shadows, seeing him stretched out so that his arms and legs took up the room I had recently occupied with him, I felt a deep something for him, something I would call tenderness for lack of a better term to name the emotion in between love and pity. But I also knew that I would not see him again. I was sixteen. I did not yet have the capability to give of myself without wanting back in full measure. I wanted romance without imperfections, passion without scars. Pito had awakened my body to its sexual potential with his hands and his mouth, and with his crazy poetry in two languages: that of war and that of love. He had taught me the geography of pleasure. Because he had given this gift, I had really meant it when I knelt by his bed and kissed him on the mouth in Spanish, in the new way he had taught me. I solemnly promised him, "I will always remember you, Pito."

"*Gracias, niña,*" he had answered in a bitter tone, turning his face toward the wall, crossing his arms over his chest protectively as if I had offered him yet another medal to pin on his wounded flesh.

The Year of Our Revolution

Mary Ellen

When my senior year began, I was immersed in politics, passion, and poetry; the three P's. All of them embodied in my boy-poet, Gerald. Gerald introduced me to protest music and the poems of Allen Ginsberg, which had a heady effect on both of us. Gerald also introduced me to my best friend in those days, his sister Gail, who once took off her clothes during a peace rally and was arrested for indecent exposure. It wasn't so much exhibitionism that prompted her to remove her blouse in front of city hall; it was love of life—an exuberance I envied.

At home and at Larry Reyes's restaurant, where my parents worked, time stood still. The Cubans talked of returning to their island and plotted the overthrow of Fidel Castro. They competed with each other in their stories of lost riches, of glamorous lives lived in tropical splendor before *La Revolución*. All of them had apparently been doctors, lawyers, socialites and descendants of Spanish aristocracy. Now, though, they worked alongside the Puerto Ricans in factories and textile mills doing menial jobs. My father served them their drinks at the bar—usually Puerto Rican rum with coke, a combination called Cuba Libre—and listened patiently to their weepy tales of lost glory. There was little else he could do for his Cuban *compañeros*. For our people, however, he could do more: He could spend his own money on them because they were his Island brothers and sisters. People knew how soft he was, and he became our barrio's father confessor and social worker, with Puerto Habana as his dispensary. My mother did what she could to help him in his mission. We stayed poor while Larry Reyes grew rich.

But my world was larger than the barrio. I kept in touch with *my* revolution through the air waves. I took my tiny transistor radio everywhere with me. The New York City DJ, Murray the K, hissed or shouted in my ear. He introduced me to the music of Aretha Franklin, Grace Slick and the Jefferson Airplane, Bob Dylan, Marvin Gaye, Santana, Joan Baez, Jimi Hendrix—the mixed-bag he called *our* rock and roll in an intimate whisper, making it sound as if he were talking about having sex. I remember I had been in the tub listening to his show when I'd first heard the Beatles' *Sgt. Pepper's Lonely Hearts Club Band.* I'd slipped down into the water, up to my ears in ecstasy, wanting to drown in sound. Joplin's wails of pain and pleasure made my extremities tingle. When I saw her picture, I couldn't believe how plain she was. But later I saw her perform on TV and witnessed the miracle that music effected on her. When she was deep into a song, Janis became beautiful. Her voice, hoarse and choked with pain, went right through my skin, and I began to understand the meaning of soul, *el duende,* in American music.

Gerald introduced me to sensuality rather than to sex. He practiced Yoga, transcendental meditation, and the art of massage. He decided that passivity and self-denial were the keys to Nirvana. His thing was for us to sit facing each other in his darkened room while he recited his poems to me. They were mainly chants of words that made his soul vibrate, he explained to me—like the strings of a celestial harp.

"Let's lap the cosmos," he'd whisper hoarsely, his mouth half an inch from mine as we sat on his imitation Persian rug: Our legs wrapped around each other, our arms intertwined, our torsos not touching. This position generated the necessary tension that inspired Gerald's verse.

"Lick the stars, stoke my fire, cross the universe on a white horse, swim the Ganges with me."

The images were enough for me. I could listen to his strings of beautiful nonsense all night. I knew it was a love poem in secret code. When Gerald ran out of poetry, he would chant to me: "Om Ah Hum," the tip of his tongue tickling my ear. "Om Ah Hum."

Then we'd get the perfumed oil out of his bag. He always had his essential supplies with him; you never knew when someone might need the magic touch. I would take off my poncho, unbutton my blouse, which was usually a diaphanous Indian cotton creation with little mirrors sewn into it and other symbolic decorations I had added. Gerald liked to guess what each patch was, each embroidered clue to my soul, by just feeling it in the dark.

"Here's comes the sun," he would say, tracing the design over my left breast, "and here is a daisy," his fingertips following each petal of the flower. Then he'd move his hand towards my nipple under the material: "And here is Mary Ellen, Mary Ellen, Mary Ellen, daughter of sun and moon, child of heaven."

He never saw me undressed, but his fingers knew my body. Gerald's Eastern philosophy and his massages in the dark were the erotic pinnacle for me that year.

There was a darker side to Gerald too, and it finally became clear to me, and to Gail, that he was modeling himself on the self-destructive figures that we injected into our unconscious, taking the words of their songs and the needle-sharp notes of their music directly into our veins. Like Hendrix, like Joplin, like Morrison, Gerald became obsessed with death as the ultimate trip. It frightened me when he first suggested that we try a peyote button. He didn't insist when I refused, but I could tell when he'd been reinforcing his mellow grass highs. No longer gentle in the way he touched me, his nails once cut into my flesh. Another time he almost choked me, his fingers locking around my throat until I pried them loose. Frightened, I left Gerald still sitting in the lotus position, staring straight ahead as if catatonic.

The next day he insisted he did not remember hurting me. I showed him the purple marks on my neck, which I had to carefully conceal at home and at school by wearing a turtleneck sweater. He cried and begged me to forgive him. I saw him a few more times, but he was turning inward for company, turning on more often, dropping out of most of his relationships. Gail and I discussed what was happening to Gerald.

"My brother is *into himself* now," Gail told me in her room, where a life-size poster of Morrison, naked to just below the waist, gazed down at us from the ceiling. She admitted to indulging in "groovy" sexual fantasies involving the sexy lead singer for the Doors;

his drug-droopy eyes were a dangerous black pool a girl could drown in, and the inviting parted lips a natural wonder to explore. His tight leather pants did not leave much to the imagination, and that was fine. We both knew what Jim Morrison could offer a girl.

"Touch Me" was playing on Gail's turntable, loudly, for privacy while we talked. Downstairs, her mother was baking an apple-cinnamon pie for Gerald, trying to bring him back from his cosmic travels with the aromas of her kitchen. Gerald's father had scarcely spoken to his son for almost two years, since they had driven together into a gas station and the attendant had innocently called his long-haired, pretty son "Miss." Gerald, Sr. had turned the car around, walked back into the house and announced to his wife that the creature wearing a clown suit and beads was not his son anymore.

There had been scenes, tears and misguided attempts at compromise by the well-meaning mother, all of which were met by her son's passive resistance. Her pleas and threats were sometimes rewarded with a sweet kiss and vacant eyes, a flower from her own garden, or the flashing of a "V" for peace. Gerald's spaciness and her husband's silent hostility had almost defeated her. She had at first turned to Gail for comfort, but instead of her darling little girl, she had found a fledgling women's libber and flower-child. Gail suggested to her mother that she leave her square husband and "turn on to life." According to Gail, her mother had instead joined a Bible study group and a bridge club, where other exiled mothers and wives compared their children's terrorist activities and prayed that this rebellious phase turned national epidemic would pass during their lifetimes.

"What do you mean Gerald's *into himself*," I asked Gail. I was feeling resentful about Gerald's new indifference, which he said was really "peaceful acceptance" on his part. This translated to: If I wanted to see him, fine, I could find him; if I didn't want to see him, fine, he would be doing the same thing anyway: getting stoned, listening to "In-a-Gadda-Da-Vida" with the turntable's arm in the up position so that the record album would play continuously without interruption until Gerald left the room and his patient mother came and turned the thing off. The father had bought earplugs.

"Well, Mary Ellen, what it means to Gerald," Gail said, turning to face me on the narrow single bed where we were both stretched out together, almost falling off the sides, "is that he doesn't care about *this* anymore." Catching me off-guard, she pinched my nipple, giggling uncontrollably while I rubbed it. I fell halfway off the bed still managing to give her the finger in outrage.

"Are you on something, girl?"

"I'm high on life, E-le-ni-ta," she said still laughing, enunciating my Spanish name syllable by syllable.

"I want to know what's up with Gerald. Can you get serious?"

"I can tell you what's *not* up with my brother." She laughed again, pointing to Morrison's crotch above us.

"I'm going," I said, tired of her sexual innuendos.

Gail had joined a women's awareness-raising group her first term at City College, and their "thing" was to treat sex as an open topic, to expand their horizons by trying "everything" sexually, which meant that your friends and neighbors were all fair game as potential partners in your choice of adventures. Until the nipple-tweaking impulse had overtaken Gail, I'd felt that as her brother's girlfriend I had safe passage, or diplomatic sexual immunity, around Gail. Apparently, now that Gerald was "into himself"—no longer interested in exploring the universe in my company—Gail had felt she could cross the line.

"Don't be afraid of me, Mary Ellen," Gail's tone turned serious as she gently placed her hand on my shoulder, pulling me back down next to her on the bed. "At this very moment, maybe because I was thinking of the last time Gerald—you know, gave you a massage, I did feel turned on. But I can be cool about it. We can talk."

"How do you know . . . I mean . . . did Gerald tell you . . ." I was shocked that Gail knew about my sessions with Gerald. I had always told her about the poetry and the massages, but, not the other stuff. In spite of my outward bravura and my rebelliousness against my parents' uptight moral values, I felt a little ashamed of letting Gerald touch me the way he did. Because we did it in total darkness in his room, I stupidly believed that no one else suspected what went on.

"I was there," Gail said in a whisper.

My impulse was to jump off the bed and run home. How could Gerald betray me this way? How could Gail call herself my friend when she was a voyeur, a pervert, spying on her best friend's and her brother's most intimate moments together? I surprised myself by just lying stock-still on the bed next to Gail. *And did you touch me too?* I did not ask aloud.

Next to me, her mouth close to my ear, Gail hummed a song we both knew, but did not move either.

Gerald emerged from his dark cocoon enough times to finish high school, although he tested and stretched the limits of Queen of Heaven High's faculty and administration. He might never have graduated if it had not been for our hippie-nun Sister Mary Joseph's intercession—and the fact that he was brilliant. He read and understood philosophy. High-school subjects were child's play to him, for Gerald could interpret the words of Shakespeare, Milton and Blake as well as those and John, Paul, George and Ringo. He couldn't have cared less about the diploma, but somehow, even in the recesses of his chemically saturated brain, he must have known that it would undo the last connection he had to his family and to the world if he did not finish his senior year. Also, he saw life as a series of events that you either allowed to happen to you or you passively resisted. He allowed his high-school graduation to happen to him, then he celebrated his freedom by blowing his mind with acid at a rock festival. The unforeseen consequence of his orgy was half a year in the nuthouse, paid for by his father's insurance company, followed by the realization that the breakdown had been a gift from the karmic forces of rock-and-roll: He would not be drafted.

Gerald's dropping-out had been gradual, though, and my memories of our senior year are like black and white photographs with a shadowy figure at the edge that no one can quite identify. That was Gerald. Gerald in his ankle-length black trench coat, John Lennon-style eyeglasses and hair down to his shoulders, standing just behind me at the café where we listened to the other young men and women in black recite their angry verses and sing their protest songs. More and more I began to lose interest in the mediocre poetry and the mindless repetition of slogans. My own pupa-stage poems were seeking out the concrete image that would years later give shape, form and meaning to my fragmented world.

My mother never met Gerald or Gail, or many of my friends outside the barrio. But she watched me from her window, and she waited and she knew, maybe through her dreams which she believed in, or by my smell, my music, by my wild look. Or maybe by spying on my sidewalk passions with Gerald. She knew that I was staring down the abyss with my boy-poet. So she gave me a choice one night: free love or her love.

કરે

María Elena

My hair started turning gray that year, seeing the turmoil on the streets of America and waiting for my daughter to come home from her rallies, demonstrations and sit-ins. Late into the night, I sat in my rocker by the window, waiting to see the pretty girl with the wild black mane of hair hiding herself inside a huge poncho. I watched her coming down the block, clutching her books and papers, head bowed as if she were burdened with the worries of the whole world. Such a serious child. So intent on righting wrongs that she missed all of the good things that I thought a young girl would want: pretty clothes, fiestas, fun with other teen-agers. I knew that she liked boys, although those years I had to look very closely to tell the difference between the sexes. Both wore the ragged blue jeans, painted t-shirts and ridiculous jewelry. They let their hair grow and wore it wild and tangled as moss on a tree. From my window I could not always tell if her occasional companions were girlfriends or *novios*.

There was no doubt, however, the night I saw the obscene kiss in front of our building. By the light of the street lamp, I could clearly see the entire spectacle. Although I did not want her to know that I watched her in such a clandestine manner, I was alarmed one night to see the groping and abandoned caresses. It was *el poeta*, Gerald, she wrapped herself around one night. The boy looked like he needed a good night's sleep, a hot meal and a hair-brush. I did not understand what she saw in him. Perhaps her enchantment with words and poetry was embodied in the unkempt boy. I knew I had to say something to her about the display on the street. She walked in preceded by the wave of that patchouli oil that permeated her person and everything she touched in those days. It was a pagan smell, calling up for me images of naked people dancing around a fire. I was sitting in the dark living room, so I startled her when I spoke her name.

"Elenita. Please come here for a minute, *niña*," I said, trying to calm myself before speaking.

"What are you doing up so late, Mother? Hey, have you been spying on me?"

"*I* will ask the questions, Elenita." I reached over and turned on the light. Her hands shot up to cover her face as if she had something to hide. But she regained her rebel pose quickly.

"Have you thought about what people in this barrio will say if they see you being intimate with a man right on the sidewalk?"

"You *were* spying on me!"

She was furious, as I knew she would be, but I was determined to speak my thoughts.

"You are forgetting something, *hija*," I spoke calmly so that she would know that I did not intend to be intimidated by her anger. "You live in my house. And as long as you as you call this home, you will answer to me and your father for your moral behavior."

"Then maybe it's time that I leave your *home*," she answered sharply. And the way she said *su casa* hurt me. "Perhaps you haven't noticed, stuck as you are behind these four walls, that there's been a sexual revolution going on out in the real world." She continued speaking in the same sarcastic tone. "People don't have to ask their parents or anyone for permission before they make love. It's a personal matter, Mother!"

"I call what you are suggesting immoral behavior, *hija*. If you are saying that for girls to pass their bodies around to many men is not a sin, then you are wrong. The body is a temple—"

"My body is *my* temple, and I will conduct services any way I want!"

I saw that I could never hope to win a battle of words with my daughter: They were her domain. Even then she could use language to her advantage like no one else I knew. So I brought out my most dangerous and final weapon. Trembling in fear, I said, "I cannot *live* with you if you have given yourself over to a life of sin. I do not want you to go, but you have become a stranger to me."

She looked at me in horror. I knew I had shocked her because she thought that my devotion to her was greater than my objections to anything she could do. And it was. I was playing this game of chance, risking my whole life and my soul—for I could no more give up my child than I could stop breathing—hoping she would understand the gravity of our moral dilemma.

"You're throwing me out?"

She had sunk to the floor in front of my rocker. Her heap of bright rags spread around her, she seemed to shrink into a little girl again. I held back my need to comfort my child, keeping my hands locked together so as not to reach out to her.

"No, Elenita," I spoke firmly although my throat felt constricted by fear. "I am telling you that if the morals we taught you mean nothing, then we are no longer a family. You must make a choice. If you want to live without rules, then you must make a life away from us. On your own."

She sank back on her knees staring at me in disbelief, as if I had suddenly turned into a monster right there in front of her. She had never known that I too could rebel against injustice.

"You don't understand, Mother. Things have changed in the world. A modern woman makes her own choices . . . She has the freedom to choose."

Now she was going to give me a lecture on free love, but I interrupted her.

"Nothing of value to your life is free, Elenita. *Nada. ¿Entiendes?* Not even love. Especially not love. Look around you. Women have always paid a high price for love. The highest price. I am telling you that if you want to be an adult, you have to learn the first lesson: Love will cost you. It is not free."

She sat there taking in my pronouncements. Not in the usual way that people process things. Not *my* Elenita. She was translating and transforming what I had said inside that unknowable mind of hers. And when I would hear my own words again, coming out of her mouth, they would sound foreign to me.

My plan was to walk out on *her* for once, leaving her there to think about the choices I had given her. But I could not help myself. As I walked past my *niña* sitting stiffly in her pagan costume, I stroked her hair. She lay her wild head inside the circle of my arms for one brief moment, then rushed to her room to drown out the world with her long-playing albums. I will remember that night as the beginning of the end of the worst year in the history of parents and children: 1968, the year of our revolution.

María Sabida

Once upon a time there lived a girl who was so smart that she was known throughout Puerto Rico as María Sabida. María Sabida came into the world with her eyes open. They say that at the moment of her birth she spoke to the attending midwife and told her what herbs to use to make a special *guarapo*, a tea that would put her mother back on her feet immediately. They say that the two women would have thought the infant was possessed if María Sabida had not convinced them with her descriptions of life in heaven that she was touched by God and not spawned by the Devil.

María Sabida grew up in the days when the King of Spain owned Puerto Rico, but had forgotten to send law and justice to this little island lost on the map of the world. And so thieves and murderers roamed the land, terrorizing the poor people. By the time María Sabida was of marriageable age, one such *ladrón* had taken over the district where she lived.

For years people had been subjected to abuse from this evil man and his henchmen. He robbed them of their cattle and then made them buy their own cows back from him. He would take their best chickens and produce when he came into town on Saturday afternoons, riding with his men through the stalls set up by farmers. Overturning their tables, he would yell, "Put it on my account." But of course he never paid for anything he took. One year several little children

The Year of Our Revolution

disappeared while walking to the river, and although the townspeople searched and searched, no trace of them was ever found. That is when María Sabida entered the picture. She was fifteen then, and a beautiful girl with the courage of a man, they say.

She watched the chief *ladrón* the next time he rampaged through the *pueblo*. She saw that he was a young man: red-skinned, and tough as leather. *Cuero y sangre, nada más,* she said to herself, a man of flesh and blood. And so she prepared herself to either conquer or to kill this man.

María Sabida followed the horses' trail deep into the woods. Though she left the town far behind she never felt afraid or lost. María Sabida could read the sun, the moon, and the stars for direction. When she got hungry, she knew which fruits were good to eat, which roots and leaves were poisonous, and how to follow the footprints of animals to a waterhole. At nightfall, María Sabida came to the edge of a clearing where a large house, almost like a fortress, stood in the forest.

"No woman has ever set foot in that house," she thought, "no *casa* is this, but a man-place." It was a house built for violence, with no windows on the ground level, but there were turrets on the roof where men could stand guard with guns. She waited until it was nearly dark and approached the house through the kitchen side. She found it by smell.

In the kitchen, which she knew would have to have a door or window for ventilation, she saw an old man stirring a huge pot. Out of the pot stuck little arms and legs. Angered by the sight, María Sabida entered the kitchen, pushed the old man aside, and picking up the pot threw its horrible contents out of the window.

"Witch, witch, what have you done with my master's stew!" yelled the old man. "He will kill us both when he gets home and finds his dinner spoiled."

"Get, you filthy *viejo*." María Sabida grabbed the old man's beard and pulled him to his feet. "Your master will have the best dinner of his life if you follow my instructions."

María Sabida then proceeded to make the most delicious *asopao* the old man had ever tasted, but she would answer no questions about herself, except to say that she was his master's fiancée.

When the meal was done, María Sabida stretched and yawned and said that she would go upstairs and rest until her *prometido* came home. Then she went upstairs and waited.

The men came home and ate ravenously of the food María Sabida had cooked. When the chief *ladrón* had praised the old man for a fine meal, the cook admitted that it had been *la prometida* who had made the tasty chicken stew.

"My what?" the leader roared, "I have no *prometida*." And he and his men ran upstairs. But there were many floors, and by the time they were halfway to the room where María Sabida waited, many of the men had dropped down unconscious, and the others had slowed down to a crawl, until they too were overcome with irresistible sleepiness. Only the chief *ladrón* made it to where María Sabida awaited him holding a paddle that she had found among his weapons. Fighting to keep his eyes open, he asked her, "Who are you, and why have you poisoned me?"

"I am your future wife, María Sabida, and you are not poisoned, I added a special sleeping powder that tastes like oregano to your *asopao*. You will not die."

"Witch!" yelled the chief *ladrón* "I will kill you. Don't you know who I am?" And reaching for her, he fell on his knees, whereupon María Sabida beat him with the paddle until he lay curled like a child on the floor. Each time he tried to attack her, she beat him some more. When she was satisfied that he was vanquished, María Sabida left the house and went back to town.

A week later, the chief *ladrón* rode into town with his men again. By then everyone knew what María Sabida had done and they were afraid of what these evil men would do in retribution. "Why did you not just kill him when you had a chance, *muchacha*?" many of the townswomen had asked María Sabida. But she had just answered mysteriously, "It is better to conquer than to kill." The townspeople then barricaded themselves behind closed doors when they heard the pounding of the thieves' horses approaching. But the gang did not stop until they arrived at María Sabida's house. There the men, instead of guns, brought out musical instruments: a *cuatro*, a *güiro*, *maracas,* and a harmonica. Then they played a lovely melody.

"María Sabida, María Sabida, my strong and wise María," called out the leader, sitting tall on his horse under María Sabida's window, "come out and listen to a song I've written for you—I call it *The Ballad of María Sabida*."

Judith Ortiz Cofer

María Sabida then appeared on her balcony wearing a wedding dress. The chief *ladrón* sang his song to her: a lively tune about a woman who had the courage of a man and the wisdom of a judge, who had conquered the heart of the best *bandido* on the island of Puerto Rico. He had a strong voice, and all the people cowering in their locked houses heard his tribute to María Sabida and crossed themselves at the miracle she had wrought.

One by one they all came out, and soon María Sabida's front yard was full of people singing and dancing. The *ladrones* had come prepared with casks of wine, bottles of rum, and a wedding cake made by the old cook from the tender meat of coconuts. The leader of the thieves and María Sabida were married on that day. But all had not yet been settled between them. That evening, as she rode behind him on his horse, she felt the dagger concealed beneath his clothes. She knew then that she had not fully won the battle for this man's heart.

On her wedding night María Sabida suspected that her husband wanted to kill her. After their dinner, which the man had insisted on cooking himself, they went upstairs. María Sabida asked for a little time alone to prepare herself. He said he would take a walk but would return very soon. When she heard him leave the house, María Sabida went down to the kitchen and took several gallons of honey from the pantry. She went back to the bedroom and there she fashioned a life-sized doll out of her clothes and poured the honey into it. She then blew out the candle, covered the figure with a sheet and hid herself under the bed.

After a short time, she heard her husband climbing the stairs. He tip-toed into the dark room thinking her asleep in their marriage bed. Peeking out from under the bed, María Sabida saw the glint of the knife her husband pulled out from inside his shirt. Like a fierce panther he leapt onto the bed and stabbed the doll's body over and over with his dagger. Honey splattered his face and fell on his lips. Shocked, the man jumped off the bed and licked his lips.

"How sweet is my wife's blood. How sweet is María Sabida in death—how sour in life and how sweet in death. If I had known she was so sweet, I would not have murdered her." And so declaring, he kneeled down on the floor beside the bed and prayed to María Sabida's soul for forgiveness.

At that moment María Sabida came out of her hiding place. "Husband, I have tricked you once more, I am not dead." In his joy, the man threw down his knife and embraced María Sabida, swearing that he would never kill or steal again. And he kept his word, becoming in later years an honest farmer. Many years later he was elected mayor of the same town he had once terrorized with his gang of *ladrones*.

María Sabida made a real *casa* out of his thieves' den, and they had many children together, all of whom could speak at birth. But, they say, María Sabida always slept with one eye open, and that is why she lived to be one hundred years old and wiser than any other woman on the Island of Puerto Rico, and her name was known even in Spain.

Judith Ortiz Cofer

So Much for Mañana

After twenty years on the mainland
Mother's gone back to the Island
to let her skin
melt from her bones
under her native sun.
She no longer wears stockings,
girdles or tight clothing.
Brown as a coconut,
she takes siestas in a hammock,
and writes me letters that say:
"Stop chasing your own shadow, *niña*,
come down here and taste the *piña*,
put away those heavy books,
don't you worry about your shape,
here on the Island men look
for women who can carry a little weight.
On every holy day,
I burn candles and I pray
that your brain won't split
like an avocado pit
from all that studying.
What do you say?
Abrazos from your Mamí and a blessing
from that saint, Don Antonio, *el cura*."
I write back: "Someday I will go back
to your Island and get fat,
but not now, Mamá, maybe mañana."

*E*l Olvido

It is a dangerous thing
to forget the climate of
your birthplace; to choke out
the voices of the dead relatives when
in dreams they call you by
your secret name; dangerous
to spurn the clothes you were
born to wear for the sake of fashion;
to use weapons and sharp instruments you
are not familiar with; dangerous
to disdain the plaster saints before
which your mother kneels praying for you with
embarrassing fervor that you survive in
the place you have chosen to live; a costly,
bare and elegant room with no pictures
on the walls: a forgetting place where
she fears you might die of exposure.
Jesús, María, y José.
El olvido is a dangerous thing.

About the Author

Judith Ortiz Cofer is the author of numerous award-winning books. *An Island Like You: Stories of the Barrio* received the 1995 Pura Belpré Award and was listed among both the American Library Association's Best Books for Young Adults and *Horn Book/Fanfare* Best Books of the Year. Her poetry collections include *Terms of Survival* and *Reaching for the Mainland*. Her work has appeared in such publications as *Glamour, Kenyon Review, The Norton Book of Women's Lives,* and *Best American Essays.* Her novel *The Line of the Sun* was published in 1989. In 1997, her memoir *Silent Dancing* was translated into Spanish as *Bailando en silencio: Escenas de una niñez puertorriqueña.* Born in Hormigueros, Puerto Rico, Judith Ortiz Cofer is a professor of English and creative writing at the University of Georgia in Athens.

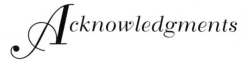

Acknowledgments

Several pieces in this volume first appeared in book form in the author's *Terms of Survival* (Arte Público Press, 1987) and *Silent Dancing: A Partial Remembrance of a Puerto Rican Childhood* (Arte Público Press, 1990); "Kennedy in the Barrio" was first published in *Microfiction: An Anthology of Really Short Stories,* edited by Jerome Stern (Norton, 1996). "Volar" was first published in *In Short: A Collection of Brief Creative Nonfiction,* Judith Kitchen and Mary Paumier Jones, editors (Norton, 1996).